# Dr. Seuss Workbook
## PHONICS

There are few things as fun as the fabulous thrill of learning a brand-new skill!

# Let's Learn to Read!

Welcome to Dr. Seuss Workbooks, where kids learn and practice important skills they'll use in the classroom and beyond!

This book teaches reading through **phonics**, which helps children match written letters and spoken sounds.

Your child will learn to read words by putting together sounds, either from single letters or word chunks.

Along the way, they will also learn many **sight words.**

Sight words are words you learn to recognize by sight. Some of these are important words that might not follow the rules of spelling and may not be easy to recognize just by putting together letter sounds.

On some pages, you'll see this icon. It indicates a place where your child is encouraged to read out loud. Help them get comfortable matching letters with sounds. That's phonics!

See it, say it!

We hope your child has tons of fun with these activities as they play, laugh...and read!

—Your friends at Dr. Seuss

now we play

# Don't Forget the Alphabet!

Follow the trail. Write the correct letter in each blank space. The first one has been done for you.

As you write each letter, say the word out loud.

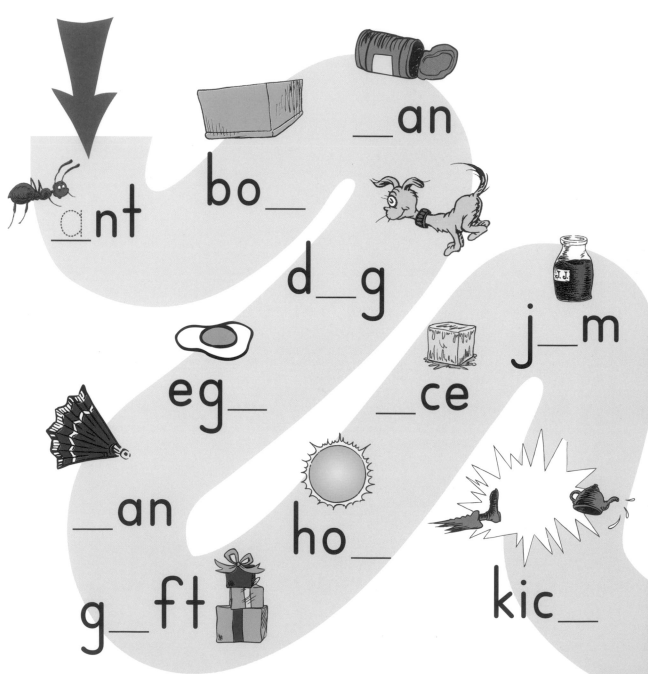

_an

bo_

_ant

d_g

eg_

j_m

_ce

_an

ho_

g_ft

kic_

4

_ot

quac__

sl_g

p_g

tal_

va__e

_ld

_p

_hale

ne__

-ray

mi__k

y_ll

_amp

za__

# Review Short Vowels A and E

The word **hat** has a **short a** sound in the middle.
The word **bed** has a **short e** sound in the middle.

Write the letter **a** or **e** to finish each word, then say
the word aloud.

h__n          b__g

c__p     p__t     r__t

**See it,
say it!**

What sound does the **short a** make?
Say it three times.

# Circle four things that have a **short a** sound.

# Draw something that has the **short e** sound.

# Review Short Vowels
# I and O

The word **hit** has a **short i** sound in the middle.
The word **hot** has a **short o** sound in the middle.

Write the letter **i** or **o** to finish each word, then say
the word aloud.

t_p          p_t          s_t

h_p          p_g          f_x

Draw a path from each picture to the matching word that has a **short i** sound.

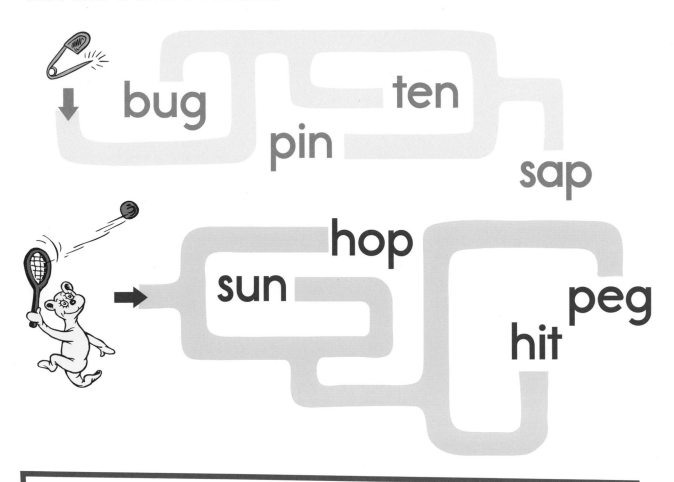

Draw something that has the **short o** sound.

# It's a U Review

The word **cub** has a **short** u sound in the middle.

Write the letter **u** to finish each word, then say the word aloud.

c__t    f__n    r__n

b__g    p__p    s__n

Find a path from **START** to **END**. You can only go through words that have the **short u** sound.

START

gum

hill

hop

hit

tug

fun

sit

slug

peg

nap

but

dog

pen

rug

cap

run

hat

top

pan

sit

big

wig

can

ran

nip

bit

hat

mug

bag

tip

pig

bin

rub

cup

hut

cat

END

11

# Words with S and Y

Circle four things that end in the letter y.

Add the letter s to the end of each word to make it **plural.**

bottle__    duck__

star__    apple__

Circle all the words that contain the letters **y** or **s**.

can    sunny    hot

pig    care

any    no

cat

many    his

silly    cars    hen

Look at the words above. Write the two words you found that contain *both* **y** and **s**.

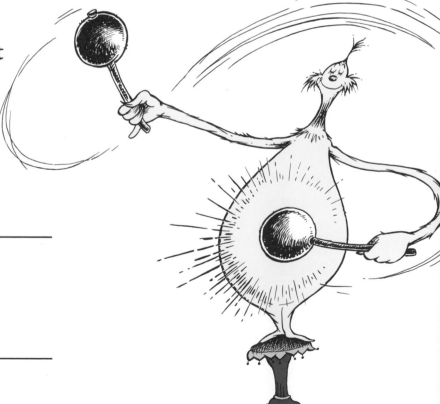

_____

_____

# Sight Words

Color each of these new sight words.

come for with out into been

Write each word and say it aloud.

**See it, say it!**

_____   _____

_____   _____

_____   _____

Draw a line between each matching word.

| | |
|---|---|
| come | into |
| for | out |
| into | for |
| out | been |
| with | come |
| been | with |

Cross out the ones that are not real words.

out

tmex

for

plyp

come

binl

been

into

noow

with

# Word Fun

Trace each line and write the word the letters make in the space at the end.

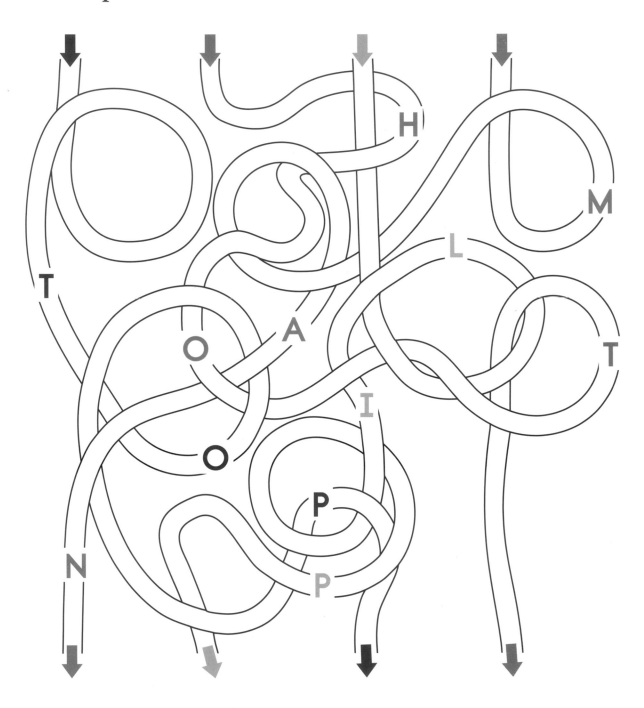

_____    _____    _____    _____

# Unscramble the letters and write the word next to each picture.

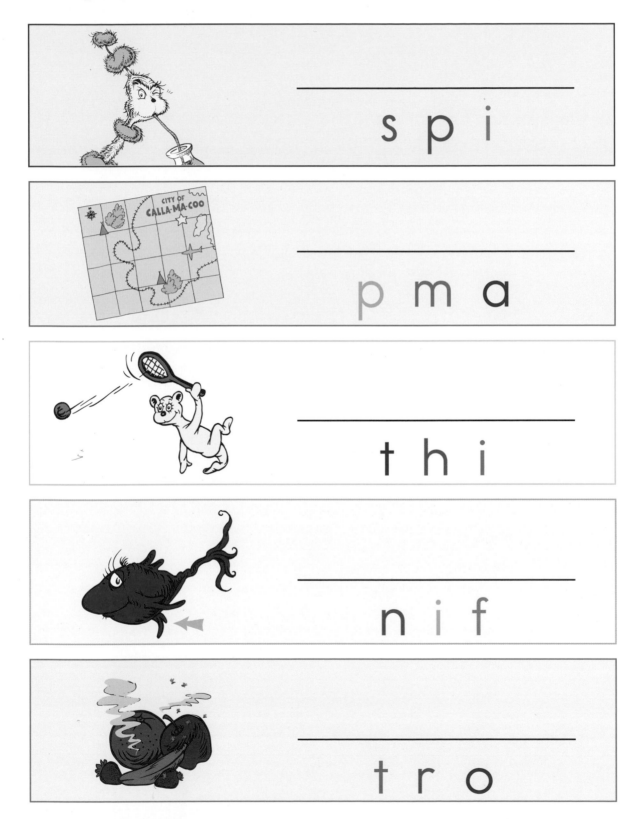

_____

s p i

_____

p m a

_____

t h i

_____

n i f

_____

t r o

# A Review for You!

Trace each line. Write the words the letters make.

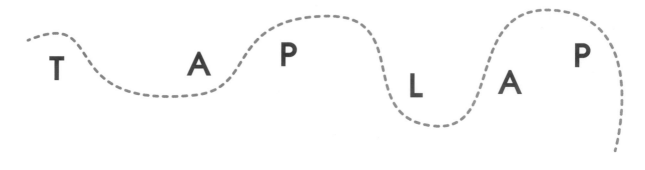

T    A    P        L    A    P

____  ____        ____  ____

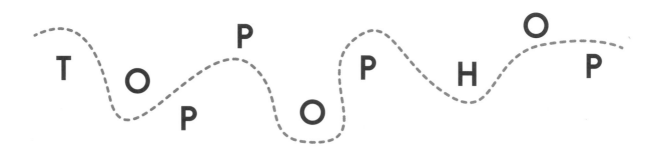

T    O    P        P    O    P        H    O    P

____  ____  ____        ____  ____  ____        ____  ____  ____

T    H    E        B    I    G        P    I    G

____  ____  ____        ____  ____  ____        ____  ____  ____

**See it, say it!**    Say each word aloud.

18

Circle all the words that contain the letters **at**.

The man sat by me.

The cat was with a bug.

The rat can come into the hut.

Look at that thing.

His hat is brown.

The bat can fly.

**See it, say it!**

Read each sentence above.
You can do it!

19

# Meet Silent Letter E

The words **cake** and **rope** have a silent letter **e** at the end.

Write the letter **e** to finish each word, then say the word aloud.

## man__

## lat__

## bik__

## can__

**See it, say it!** Say **cap** and **cape** three times. How does the **silent e** change things?

20

# Circle four things that have a **silent e.**

Draw something that has the letter **o** and ends with a **silent e.**

# Explore More Es

The words **bite** and **cube** also have a **silent letter e** at the end.

Write the letter **e** to finish each word, then say the world aloud.

tub__

tun__

kit__

rid__

Draw a path from each picture to the matching word that ends in a **silent e**.

dunk

cart

wink

pine

vase

film

top

milk

step

sun

cube

cup

# Silent Es Everywhere

The words **home**, **time**, and **dune** all end in a **silent e**.

Write **e** to finish each word.

ros__

cak__

mul__

bit__

bab__

ap__

# Find a path from START to END. You can only go through words that have a **silent e**.

**START**

bake    hole    page    mile    sale

tent    line

met    look    ten    sell    mad

bed    rag

bag    seed

mug

rat

set    met    sun

bug

wed

cat    bite    beg

tile    rad

and    them    tag    bed    fell

kite

bike    mine

tree

frog

hose    net

mole

**END**

# Many Sounds with Y

The letter y in the word **candy** makes a **long e** sound.
The letter y in the word **try** makes a **long i** sound.

Write y to finish each word.

## sunn__

## sh__

## fl__

## bunn__

Circle all the words that end in y.

baby

flop

crust

happy

ship

lazy

messy

Circle the words that end in y in this puzzle. They go up, down, and across. Use the words in the word box to help you.

| dizzy | spy | busy | try |
|-------|-----|------|-----|

| S | P | Y | R | D |
|---|---|---|---|---|
| U | Y | N | G | I |
| B | U | S | Y | Z |
| Y | M | A | R | Z |
| S | O | T | T | Y |

# Sight Words

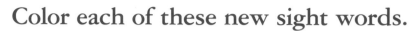

Color each of these new sight words.

him find
each all
her see

Write each word and say it aloud.

See it,
say it!

_____    _____

_____    _____

_____    _____

Draw a line between each matching word.

| | |
|---|---|
| him | all |
| find | find |
| each | see |
| all | him |
| her | each |
| see | her |

Cross out the ones that are not real words.

all
find
ith
each
her
bbr
him
crxth
see
tooorth

# Word Fun

Trace each line and write the word the letters make in the space at the end.

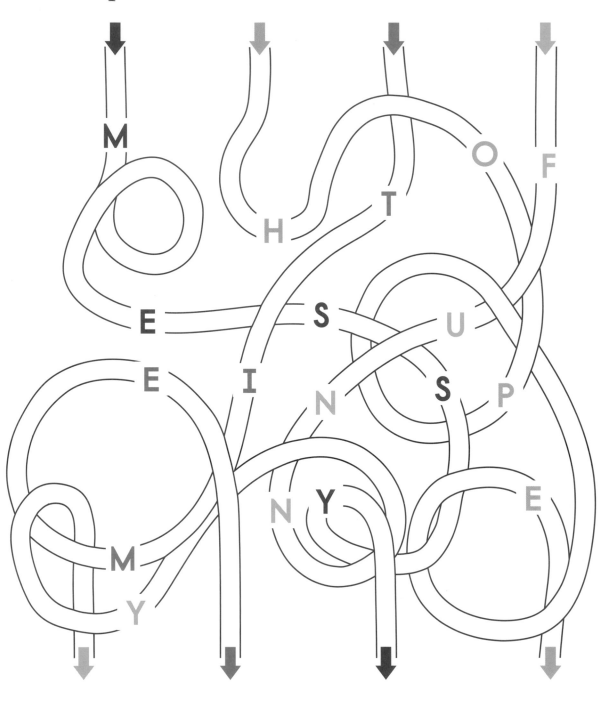

_____  _____  _____  _____

Unscramble the letters and write the word next to each picture.

_____

s l i y l

_____

e p n i

_____

s i m e l

_____

h r r u y

_____

l p o e

# A New Review!

Trace each line. Write the words the letters make.

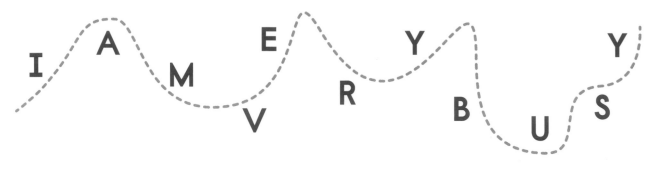

I A M E R Y B U S Y

V R

___  ___  ____  _____

_____

P

I H O E H A M

H E A S A

H E P

___  _____  ___  ___

_____  ___  ___  ____

**See it, say it!**

Say each word aloud.

Circle all the words that have a **silent e.**

My name is Dan.

I want to bake a cake.

Look at him win a race.

She rides a red bike.

He broke the vase.

The lion has a mane.

**See it, say it!**

Read each sentence above.
You can do it!

# Counting Syllables

**Man** has one **syllable**. **Many** has two **syllables**.

Say each word. Then write the number of syllables in the space beside it.

hot __

and __

hope __

pepper __

follow __

sun __

many __

sunny __

number __

work __

from __

well __

water __

tiny __

the __

moon __

# Circle four things that have two syllables.

## Give the person on the left a one-syllable name.
## Give the person on the right a two-syllable name.

_____          _____

# More Fun with Syllables

In each group, circle the word with the most **syllables**.

# Find a path from **START** to **END**. You can only go through two-syllable words.

**START**

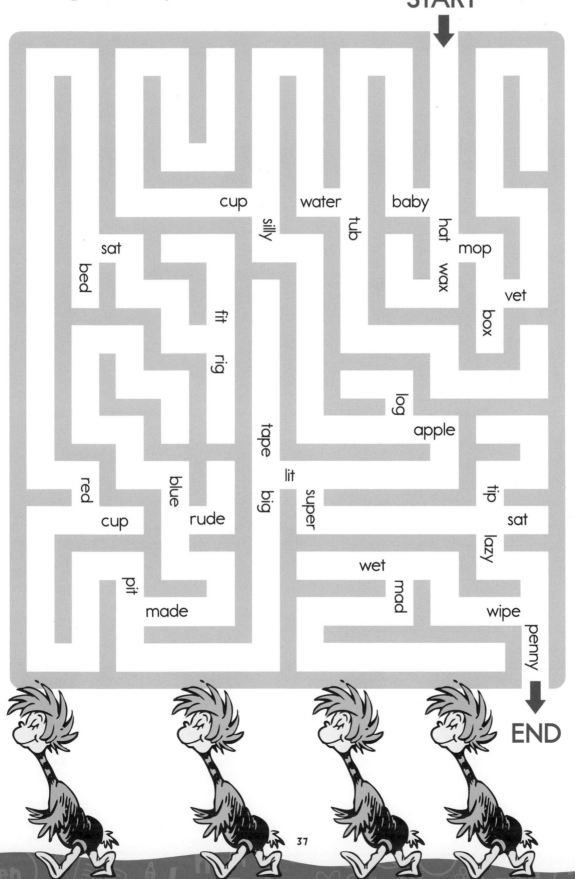

cup     water     baby

silly     tub     hat     mop

sat     wax     vet

bed     box

fit     rig

log     apple

tape     lit

red     blue     big     super     tip     sat

cup     rude     lazy

wet     mad

pit     wipe

made     penny

**END**

37

# All the Way Home

Draw a path from **START** to **END**. You can only pass through real words.

START

lpov

busy

ibbn

care

rose

zvut

zllb

lkin

date

mnook

cube

come

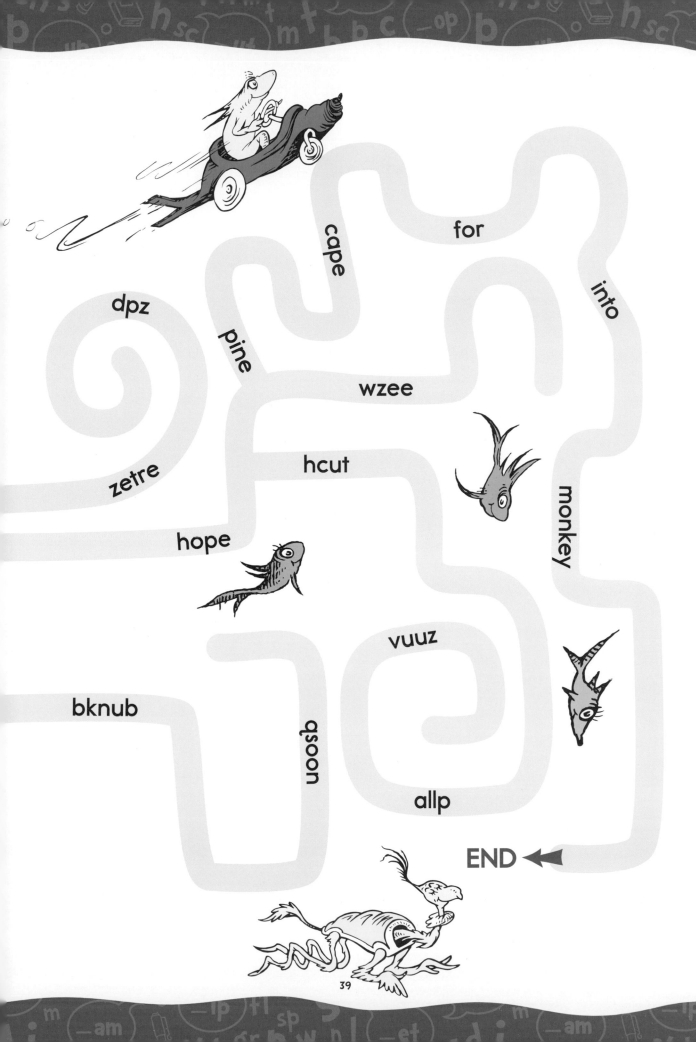

cape

for

into

dpz

pine

wzee

zetre

hcut

monkey

hope

vuuz

bknub

qsoon

allp

END ◀

# Long A Pairs

The words **rain** and **pay** both have a **long a** sound.

Write **ai** or **ay** to finish each word.

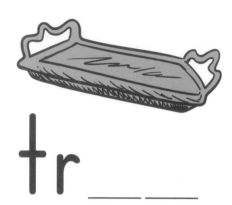

tr_____

t_____l

sn_____l

h_____

Which of these things has a **long a** sound?
Say it three times.

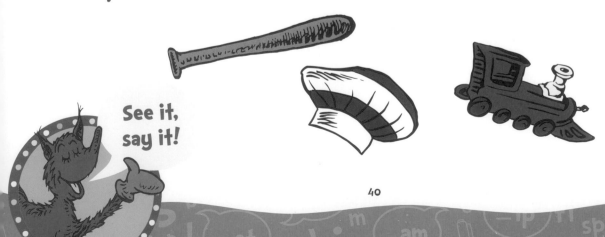

**See it, say it!**

40

# Color all the words that have a **long a** sound.

flat wait
stay
rain

Draw something that has the **long a** sound.

# Long E Pairs

The words **see** and **donkey** both have a **long e** sound.

Write **ee** or **ey** to finish each word.

monk___   qu___n

b___   k___   f___t

Which of these things has a **long e** sound?
Say it three times.

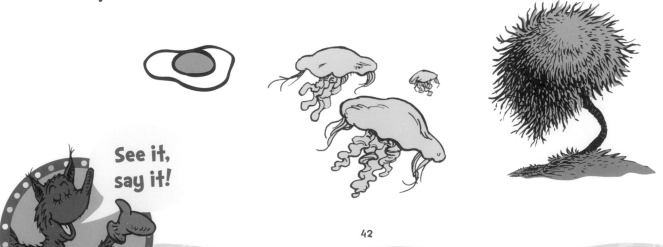

**See it,
say it!**

42

Color all the words that have a **long e** sound.

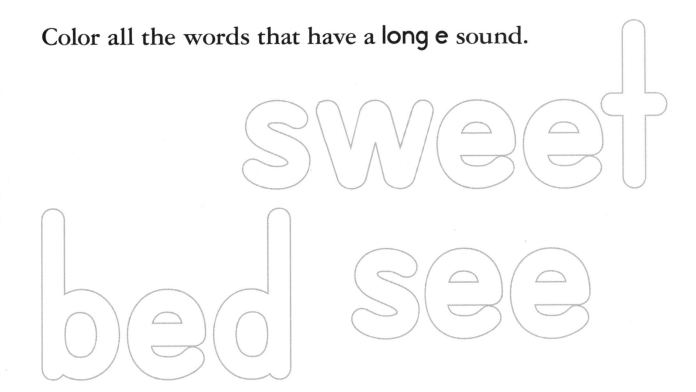

Draw a path from each picture to the matching word that has a **long e** sound.

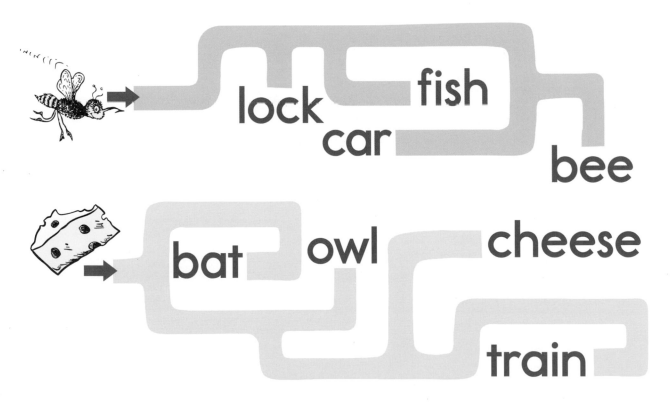

# Long O Pairs

The words **toe** and **soak** both have a **long o** sound.

Write **oe** or **oa** to finish each word.

g_ _ _t

d_ _ _

t_ _ _

b_ _ _t

Which of these things has a **long o** sound?
Say it three times.

See it, say it!

# Find a path from **START** to **END**. You can only go through words that have a **long o** sound.

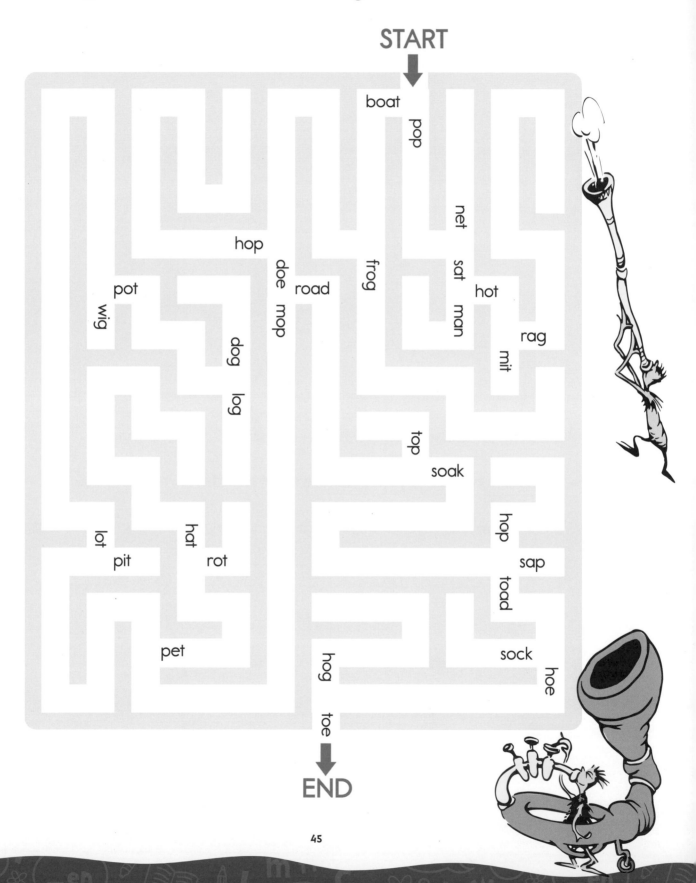

START

boat

pop

net

hop

doe  road

frog

sat  man

hot

pot

wig

doe  mop

rag

mit

dog  log

top

soak

lot

hat

hop

pit

rot

sap

toad

pet

sock

hog

hoe

toe

END

# AU and AW

The word **law** has the letters **aw**. The word **sauce** has the letters **au**. Both vowel pairs make the same sound.

Write **au** or **aw** to finish each word.

## str___

## y___n

## ___to

## p___

Circle all the words that contain the letters **au** or **aw**.

saw

wet

jaw

trap

yawn

teen

pause

sauce

cover

law

Circle the words that contain the letters **au** and **aw** in this puzzle. They go up, down, and across. Use the words in the word box to help you.

| cause | yawn | pause | paw |
|-------|------|-------|-----|

C A U S E W N

P W A R T S W

A P A U S E A

W P W W P R Y

# Look Out for IE and UE

The word **lie** has the letters **ie**. The word **blue** has the letters **ue**. Both vowel pairs make the same sound.

Write **ie** or **ue** to finish each word.

p_____

gl_____

bl_____

cl_____

t_____

fl_____s

Draw a **circle** around all the words with **ie**.
Draw a **square** around all the words with **ue**.

fries

true

lie

find

clue

lug

ties

blue

due

flood

move

same

argue

Draw a line to connect the pairs of words that rhyme.

blue                                    pie

tries                                   skies

clues                                   glues

lie                                     true

# Sight Words

Color each of these new sight words.

made

and then

part

down

Write each word and say it aloud.

**See it, say it!**

_____

_____   _____

_____   _____

Draw a line between each matching word.

| | |
|---|---|
| then | today |
| today | down |
| and | made |
| part | then |
| down | and |
| made | part |

Cross out the ones that are not real words.

and  today  nsop

lixx  typp

down  made

part

then  tweerg

# Word Fun

Trace each line. Write the words the letters make.

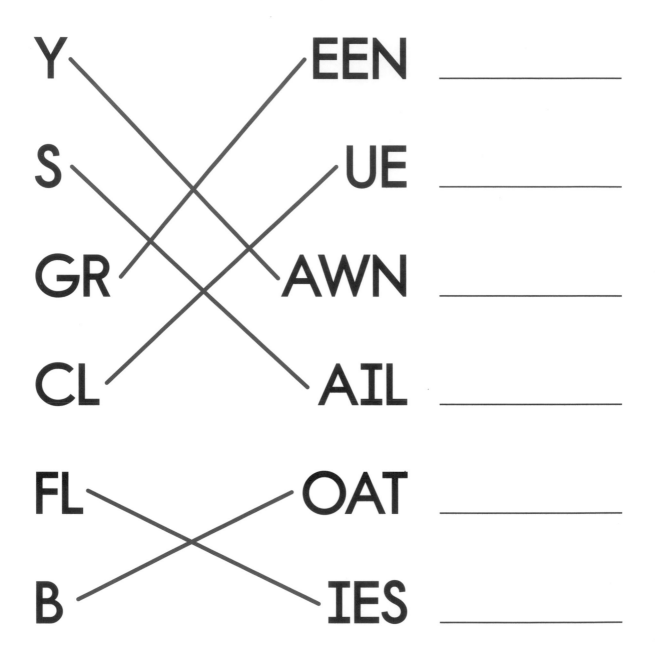

| | | |
|---|---|---|
| Y | EEN | _____ |
| S | UE | _____ |
| GR | AWN | _____ |
| CL | AIL | _____ |
| FL | OAT | _____ |
| B | IES | _____ |

**See it, say it!**

Say each word aloud.

Unscramble the letters and write the word next to each picture.

_____

e b l u

_____

n a t i r

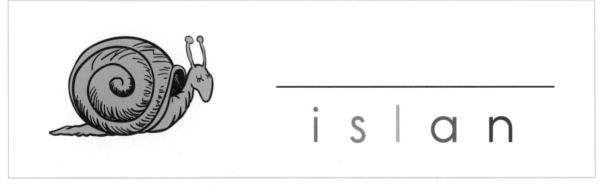

_____

i s l a n

_____

n o w c l

# A New Review!

Trace each line. Write the words the letters make.

SAY DAY PLAY

_____ _____ _____

FEEL KEYS EE

_____ _____ __

CLOWN NOSE

_____ _____

**See it, say it!**

Say each word aloud.

**Circle all the words that contain the letters ie and ue.**

Today I can bake a pie.

Now I see a blue star.

He flies up and down.

Glue all the parts.

The story is true.

She always tries.

See it, say it!

Read each sentence above.
You can do it!

# Hard and Soft C

In the word **can**, the letter **c** makes a **hard** sound.
In the word **pencil**, the letter **c** makes a **soft** sound.

Write the letter **c** to finish each word, then say the word aloud.

__arrot          __ircle

__elery          __orn

Circle the words that have a **soft c** sound.

rice     pink     creep

cast     face         nice

cup          space

# Circle four things that have a **hard c** sound.

Draw something that has a **hard c** sound.

# Hard and Soft G

In the word **gap**, the letter **g** makes a **hard** sound.
In the word **gem**, the letter **g** makes a **soft** sound.

Write the letter **g** to finish each word, then say the word aloud.

oran__e

__lue

fro__

__oat

__iraffe

__em

Draw a path from each picture to the matching word that has a **hard g** sound.

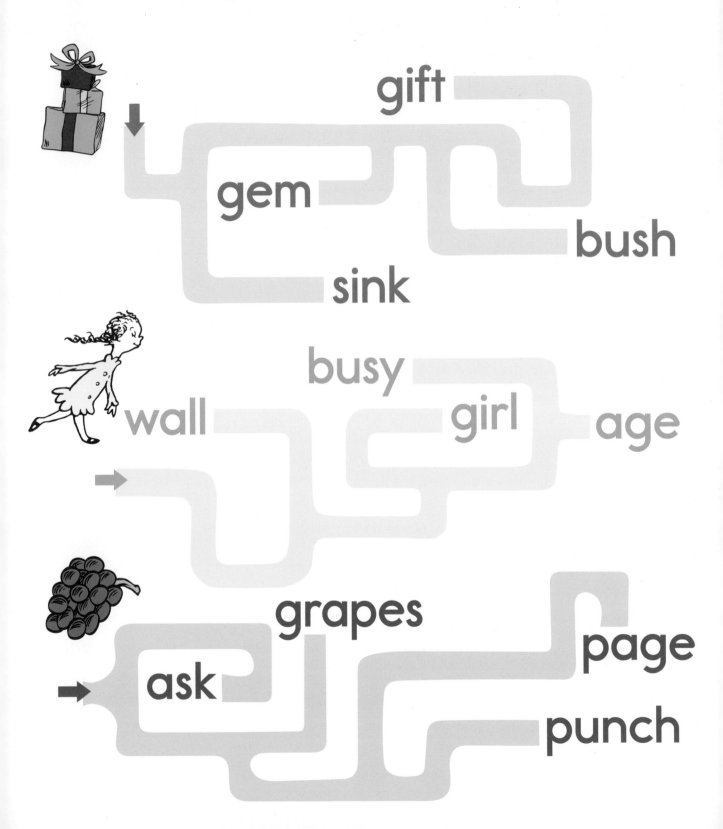

gift

gem

bush

sink

busy

wall

girl

age

grapes

page

ask

punch

# The Sounds of OW

In the words **clown** and **glow**, the letters **ow** make different sounds.

Write **ow** to finish each word.

fl____er        c____

sn____        sh____er

**See it, say it!**

Say each word aloud.

Circle all the words that have an **o** sound like **show**.

grow

now

slow

brown

power

flow

how

snow

Draw a line to connect the pairs of words that rhyme.

how                    power

shower                 now

slow                   grows

flows                  snow

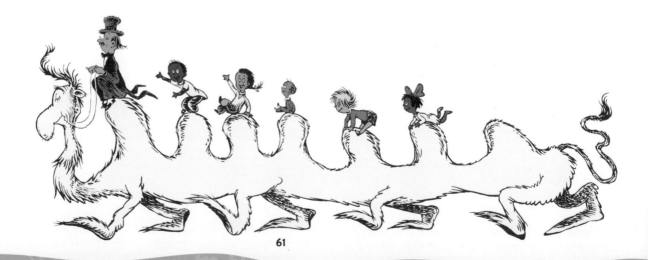

# Sight Words

Color each of these new sight words.

but why
this where
what

Write each word and say it aloud.

**See it, say it!**

_____

_____  _____

_____  _____

Draw a line between each matching word.

| | |
|---|---|
| where | what |
| but | this |
| this | but |
| why | where |
| what | why |

Cross out the ones that are not real words.

where

why

yuu     wzasl     rpy

gipp     this

snourrt     then

what

but

# Word Fun

Follow each trail and write the word the letters make in the space at the end.

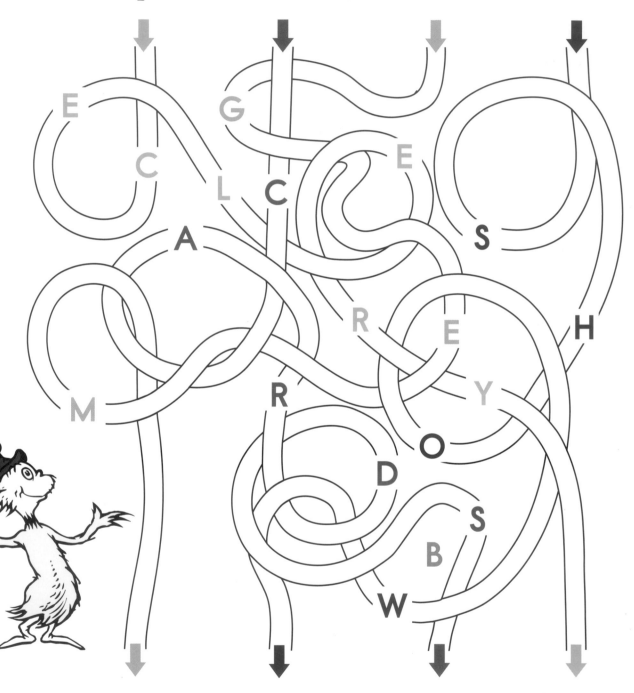

_____     _____     _____     _____

Unscramble the letters and write the word next to each picture.

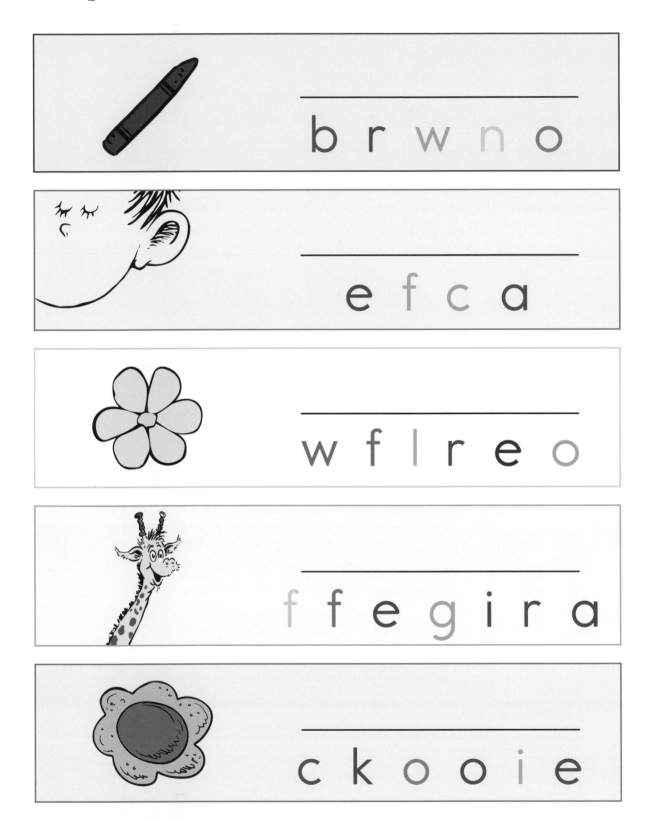

b r w n o

e f c a

w f l r e o

f f e g i r a

c k o o i e

# What's New? A Review!

Trace each line. Write the words the letters make.

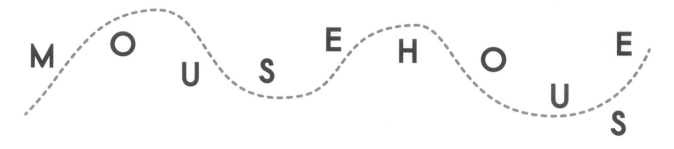

_____     _____

_____     _____

_____     _____

**See it, say it!**

Say each word aloud.

**Circle all the words that have a hard c sound.**

This is where I put my cap.

She can run fast.

We camp in a tent.

That cat can cuddle.

Cut the celery.

Carve a circle in the cement.

**See it, say it!**

Read each sentence above. You can do it!

# R Blends

The words **tray** and **free** have **blends** with the letter **r**.

Write the letters to finish each word, then say the word aloud. Use the letters in the box to help you.

| cr | fr | pr | tr | gr |
|---|---|---|---|---|

_____een

_____ee

_____own

_____og

_____esent

**See it, say it!**

Circle the letter pair that makes up the name of each object.

cr / gr

tr / pr

dr / tr

fr / cr

Draw something that contains the letters **cr**.

69

# S Blends

The words **slap** and **stay** have blends with the letter **s**.

Write the letters to finish each word, then say the word aloud. Use the letters in the box to help you.

| sl | sp | st | sm |
|---|---|---|---|

_____op

_____ug

_____ile

_____oon

**See it, say it!**

Draw a path from each picture to the matching word that begins with an **s blend**.

cover

hoop

star

think

spill

thin

sink

paper

sun

twin    raft

sled

# T Blends

The words **thin** and **try** have blends with the letter t.

Write the letters to finish each word, then say the word aloud. Use the letters in the box to help you.

| th | tr |
|----|----|

mo____

____ack

____ash

____ink

**See it, say it!**

**Find a path from START to END. You can only go through words that have th or tr in them.**

START

win
try
clown
the
up  tooth
nit
bath
sock

fix
when
red  car  nest
sled
think  fig

owl
pen
twig  slug  wig
and
moon  bee

thin
sun

fish  bug  that
fun
dog

tip
trip

END

# W Blends

The words **sweet** and **twin** have blends with the letter **w**.

Write the letters to finish each word, then say the word aloud. Use the letters in the box to help you.

| sw | tw |
|----|----|

20

____enty

____im

____eep

____ins

See it, say it!

Circle all the words that contain the letters **sw** or **tw**.

swing        rat

sweet    star          flop

tray      swift

twist         sweep

twin

Draw something that contains the letters **tw**.

# Sight Words

Color each of these
new sight words.

could

said

called

friend

Write each word and say it aloud.

**See it,
say it!**

_____    _____


_____    _____

Draw a line between each matching word.

| | |
|---|---|
| should | friend |
| could | called |
| called | said |
| friend | should |
| said | could |

Cross out the ones that are not real words.

loly     zrist     could

should

friend     efler

said

cruckyse     called

unjeeba

# Word Fun

Follow each trail and write the word the letters make in the space at the end.

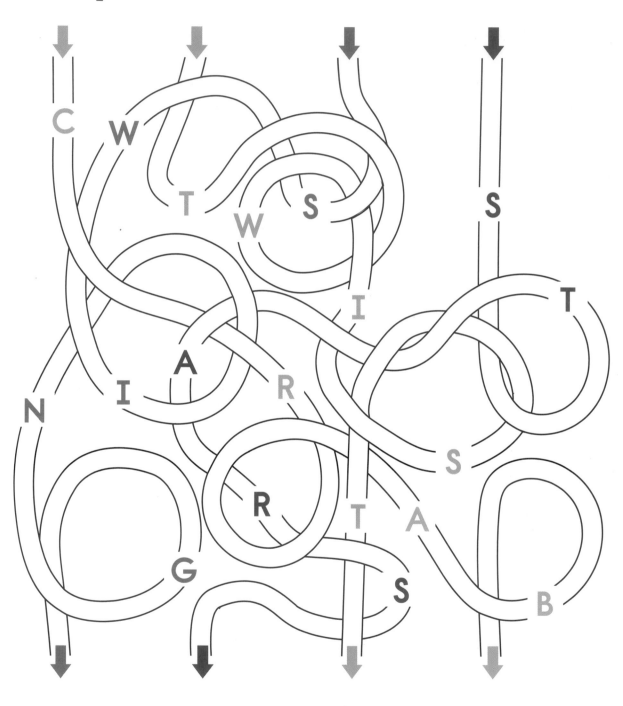

Unscramble the letters and write the word next to each picture.

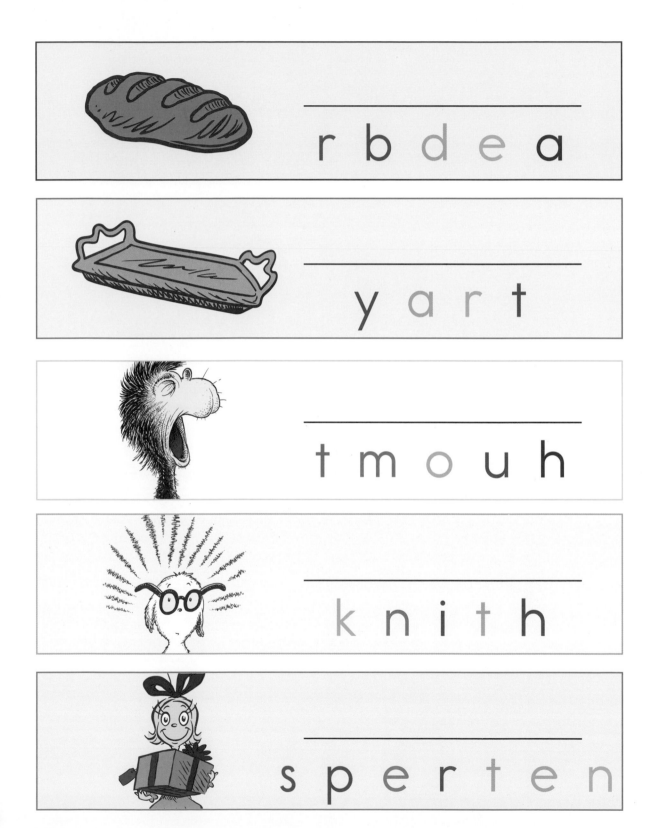

r b d e a

y a r t

t m o u h

k n i t h

s p e r t e n

# A New Review!

Trace each line. Write the words the letters make.

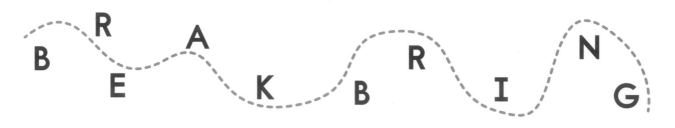

_____   _____

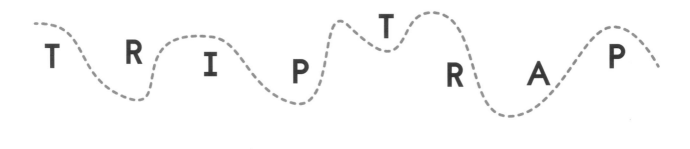

_____   _____

_____   _____

**See it, say it!**

Say each word aloud.

Circle all the words that contain **sw** or **tw**.

Could you sweep the rug?

My friend can swat a fly.

That girl has a twin.

I should fix this
twisted string.

The candy is sweet.

She likes to swing.

 Read each sentence above.
You can do it!

# CCVC Words

Clam, star, and flip are CCVC words. They have two consonants, a vowel, then one more consonant.

Write the missing vowel to finish each word, then say the word aloud.

fr_g

cr_b

pl_m

dr_m

Circle the word that has only one vowel. Say it aloud.

green    stop    clue

See it, say it!

Circle all the **CCVC** words.

clap

glue

this

then

the

flap

bee

my

and

sled

plop

drum

Draw a line to connect the pairs of words that rhyme.

drip                    drop

chap                    flip

flop                    slip

trip                    flap

# More CCVC Words

Draw a line from each word to its matching picture.

clam

flag

clip

step

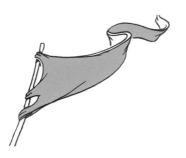

sled

crab

# Find a path from **START** to **END**. You can only go through **CCVC** words.

**START**

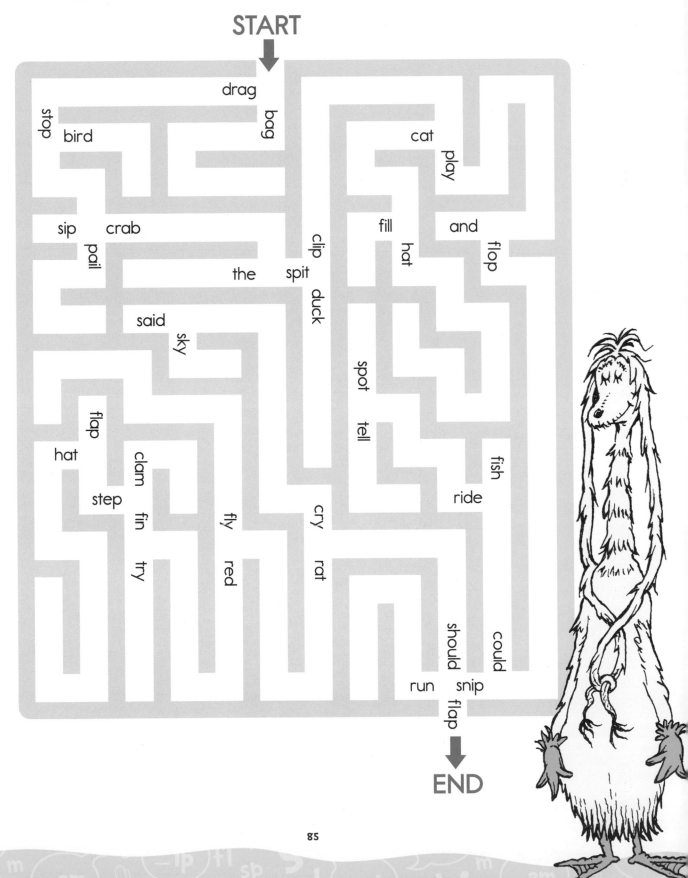

drag
bag
stop
bird
cat
play
sip crab
fill
and
pail
hat
flop
the spit
clip duck
said
sky
spot
tell
flap
fish
hat
clam fin try
step
fly red
cry rat
ride
should could
run snip
flap

**END**

# CVCC Words

Duck, lock, and pink are CVCC words. They have one consonant, a vowel, then two more consonants.

Write the two missing consonants to finish each word, then say the word aloud.

ne____          du____

li____          mi____

Circle the word that has only one vowel. Say it aloud.

fish    fire    fear

Circle all the **CVCC** words.

stop

best

clown

the

play

lock

pink

test

are

push

bird

bank

Draw a line to connect the pairs of words that rhyme.

band                              cart

part                              sent

went                              duck

tuck                              hand

# More CVCC Words

Draw a line from each word to its matching picture.

ball

fish

hump

worm

bird

wand

# Circle all the **CVCC** words.

bend    trap    sand

fold    send    drop

good    cold    gown

club    dump    stay

flag    blue    play

show    skip    crow

bird    slip

well

# Go, Go, Go!

Find a path from **START** to **END**. You can only go through real words.

**START**

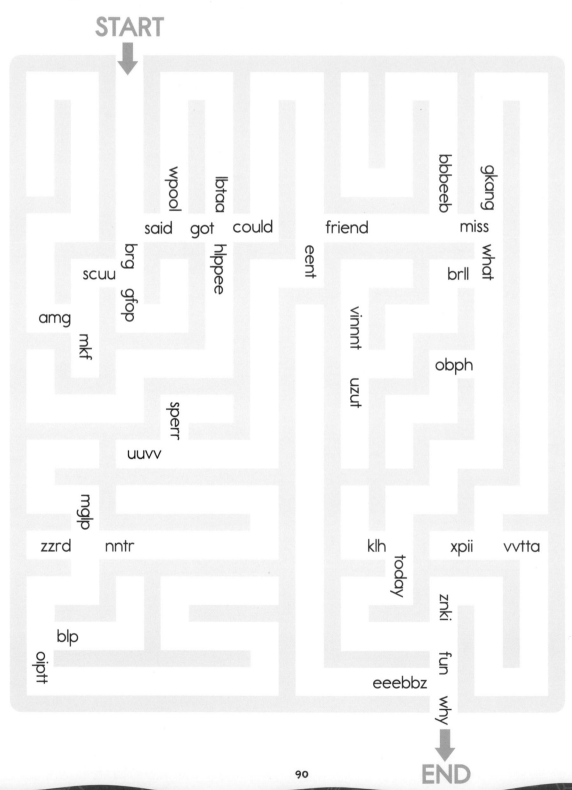

**END**

# ANSWERS

## Pages 4–5

## Pages 6–7

## Pages 8–9

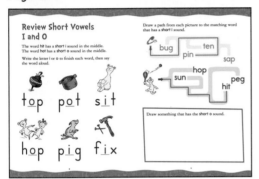

## Page 11

## Pages 12–13

## Page 15

## Pages 16–17

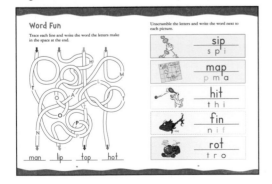

## Pages 18–19

**Page 21**

Circle four things that have a silent e.

Draw something that has the letter o and ends with a silent e.

**Page 23**

Draw a path from each picture to the matching word that ends in a silent e.

wink — cart — pine — dunk
film — top — vase
milk
step — sun — cube
cup

**Page 25**

Find a path from START to END. You can only go through words that have a silent e.

START
END

**Page 27**

Circle all the words that end in y.

baby    happy    flop
crust    ship    messy    lazy

Circle the words that end in y in this puzzle. They go up, down, and across. Use the words in the word box to help you.

| dizzy | spy | busy | try |
|---|---|---|---|

| S | P | Y | | R | | D |
| U | Y | N | G | | | I |
| B | U | S | Y | | Y | Z |
| Y | M | A | R | T | | Z |
| S | O | T | | T | | Y |

**Page 29**

Draw a line between each matching word.

him — all
find — find
each — see
all — him
her — each
see — her

Cross out the ones that are not real words.

~~hik~~    all    **find**
her    each
~~crith~~    him
see    ~~tooorth~~

**Pages 30–31**

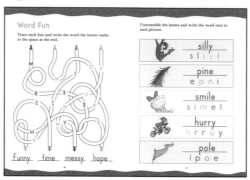

**Word Fun**

Trace each line and write the word the letters make in the space at the end.

funny    time    messy    hope

Unscramble the letters and write the word next to each picture.

silly — s l i y l
pine — e p n i
smile — s i m e l
hurry — h r r u y
pole — l p o e

**Pages 32–33**

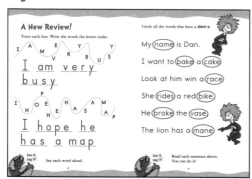

**A New Review!**

Trace each line. Write the words the letters make.

I am very busy
I hope he has a map

See it, say it! Say each word aloud.

Circle all the words that have a silent e.

My name is Dan.
I want to bake a cake.
Look at him win a race.
She rides a red bike.
He broke the vase.
The lion has a mane.

See it, say it! Read each sentence above. You can do it!

**Pages 34–35**

**Counting Syllables**

Man has one syllable. Many has two syllables.

Say each word. Then write the number of syllables in the space beside it.

hot 1    and 1
hope 1    pepper 2
follow 2    sun 1
many 2    sunny 2
number 2    work 1
from 1    well 1
water 2    tiny 2
the 1    moon 1

Circle four things that have two syllables.

Give the person on the left a one-syllable name.
Give the person on the right a two-syllable name.

**Pages 36–37**

**More Fun with Syllables**

In each group, circle the word with the most syllables.

Find a path from START to END. You can only go through two-syllable words.

START
END

**Pages 38–39**

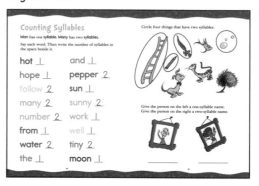

**All the Way Home**

Draw a path from START to END. You can only pass through real words.

START
END

Long A Pairs
The words rain and pay both have a long a sound.
Write ai or ay to finish each word.

tray     tail
snail    hay

Which of these things has a long a sound?
Say it three times.

Long E Pairs
The words see and donkey both have a long e sound.
Write ee or ey to finish each word.

monkey queen
bee key feet

Which of these things has a long e sound?
Say it three times.

Color all the words that have a long e sound.

# sweet
bed
see

Draw a path from each picture to the matching word that has a long e sound.

lock — fish
car
bat — owl — cheese
bee
train

Find a path from START to END. You can only go through words that have a long o sound.

START

END

Circle all the words that contain the letters au or aw.

saw   jaw   trap
yawn  wet   teen  pause
sauce cover  law

Circle the words that contain the letters au and aw in this puzzle. They go up, down, and across. Use the words in the word box to help you.

cause  yawn  pause  paw

C A U S E W N
P W A R T S W
A P A U S E A
W P W W P R Y

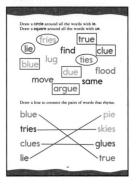

Draw a circle around all the words with ie.
Draw a square around all the words with ue.

fries  true
lie  find  clue
blue  lug  ties
due  flood
move  same
argue

Draw a line to connect the pairs of words that rhyme.

blue — pie
tries — skies
clues — glues
lie — true

Draw a line between each matching word.

then — today
today — down
and — made
part — then
down — and
made — part

Cross out the ones that are not real words.

and  today  nee
down  ~~nee~~  ~~twe~~  made
then  part

Word Fun
Trace each line. Write the words the letters make.

Y ⨯ EEN  green
S  UE  clue
GR  AWN  yawn
CL  AIL  sail
FL  OAT  boat
B  IES  flies

Say each word aloud.

Unscramble the letters and write the word next to each picture.

blue
e b l u

train
n a t i r

snail
i s l a n

clown
n o w c l

A New Review!
Trace each line. Write the words the letters make.

S A Y D A Y P L A Y
say day play

F E E L K E Y S E E
feel key see

C L O W N N O S E
clown nose

Say each word aloud.

Circle all the words that contain the letters ie and ue.

Today I can bake a pie.
Now I see a blue star.
He flies up and down.
Glue all the parts.
The story is true.
She always tries.

Read each sentence above.
You can do it!

Circle four things that have a hard c sound.

Draw something that has a hard c sound.

Draw a path from each picture to the matching word that has a hard g sound.

gift
gem
sink  bush
busy
wall  girl  age
grapes
ask  page
punch

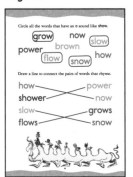

Circle all the words that have an o sound like show.

grow  now  slow
power  brown
flow  snow  how

Draw a line to connect the pairs of words that rhyme.

how — power
shower — now
slow — grows
flows — snow

Draw a line between each matching word.

where — what
but — this
this — but
why — where
what — why

Cross out the ones that are not real words.

where  why
yuu  ~~wee~~  ~~tre~~
~~gipp~~  this
what  ~~sneert~~  then
but

**Pages 64–65**

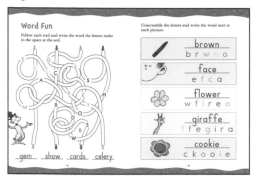

Word Fun

Follow each trail and write the word the letters make in the space at the end.

Unscramble the letters and write the word next to each picture.

brown — b r w n o
face — e f c a
flower — w f l r e o
giraffe — f f e g i r a
cookie — c k o o i e

gem    show    cards    celery

**Pages 66–67**

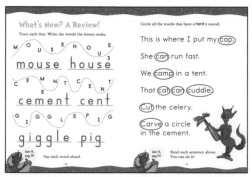

What's New? A Review!

Trace each line. Write the words the letters make.

M O U S E H O U E
mouse house
C E M N T C E N T
cement cent
G I G G L E P I G
giggle pig

Say each word aloud.

Circle all the words that have a hard c sound.

This is where I put my (cap).
She (can) run fast.
We (camp) in a tent.
That (cat) (can) (cuddle).
(Cut) the celery.
(Carve) a circle in the cement.

Read each sentence above. You can do it!

**Pages 68–69**

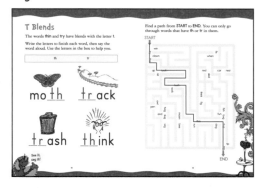

R Blends

The words tray and free have blends with the letter r.

Write the letters to finish each word, then say the word aloud. Use the letters in the box to help you.

cr    fr    pr    gr

green    tree
crown    frog
present

Circle the letter pair that makes up the name of each object.

cr / (gr)    (tr) / pr
(dr) / tr    fr / (cr)

Draw something that contains the letters cr.

**Pages 70–71**

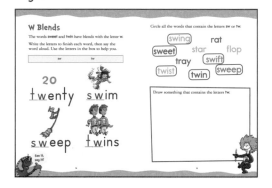

S Blends

The words slap and stay have blends with the letter s.

Write the letters to finish each word, then say the word aloud. Use the letters in the box to help you.

sl    sp    st    sm

stop    slug
smile    spoon

Draw a path from each picture to the matching word that begins with an s blend.

cover
hoop    star
think
spill
thin    sink
paper
twin    raft    sun
sled

**Pages 72–73**

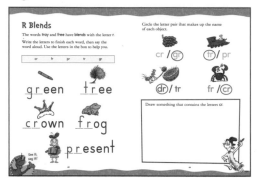

T Blends

The words thin and try have blends with the letter t.

Write the letters to finish each word, then say the word aloud. Use the letters in the box to help you.

th    tr

moth    track
trash    think

Find a path from START to END. You can only go through words that have th or tr in them.

**Pages 74–75**

W Blends

The words sweet and twin have blends with the letter w.

Write the letters to finish each word, then say the word aloud. Use the letters in the box to help you.

sw    tw

20 twenty    swim
sweep    twins

Circle all the words that contain the letters sw or tw.

(swing)    rat
(sweet)    star    flop
tray    (swift)
(twist)    (twin)    (sweep)

Draw something that contains the letters tw.

**Page 77**

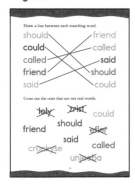

Draw a line between each matching word.

should — friend
could — called
called — said
friend — should
said — could

Cross out the ones that are not real words.

~~toly~~    ~~crist~~    could
friend    should
~~ofler~~
said    called
~~cruskyse~~    ~~unlosba~~

**Pages 78–79**

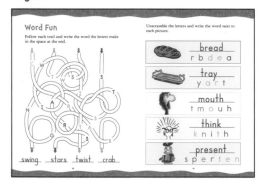

Word Fun

Follow each trail and write the word the letters make in the space at the end.

Unscramble the letters and write the word next to each picture.

bread — r b d e a
tray — y a r t
mouth — t m o u h
think — k n i t h
present — s p e r t e n

swing    stars    twist    crab

## Pages 80–81

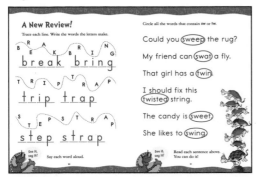

**A New Review!**

Trace each line. Write the words the letters make.

break  bring

trip  trap

step  strap

*See it, say it!* Say each word aloud.

Circle all the words that contain **sw** or **tw**.

Could you (sweep) the rug?

My friend can (swat) a fly.

That girl has a (twin).

I should fix this (twisted) string.

The candy is (sweet).

She likes to (swing).

*See it, say it!* Read each sentence above. You can do it!

## Pages 82–83

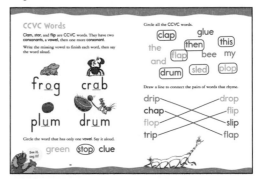

**CCVC Words**

**Clam**, **star**, and **flip** are CCVC words. They have two **consonants**, a **vowel**, then one more **consonant**.

Write the missing vowel to finish each word, then say the word aloud.

fr**o**g  cr**a**b

pl**u**m  dr**u**m

Circle the word that has only one **vowel**. Say it aloud.

green  (stop)  clue

Circle all the CCVC words.

(clap)  glue
the  (then)  (this)
and  (flap)  bee  my
(drum)  (sled)  (plop)

Draw a line to connect the pairs of words that rhyme.

drip — slip
chap — flap
flop — drop
trip — flip

## Pages 84–85

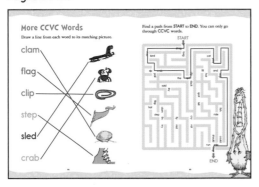

**More CCVC Words**

Draw a line from each word to its matching picture.

clam
flag
clip
step
sled
crab

Find a path from **START** to **END**. You can only go through CCVC words.

## Pages 86–87

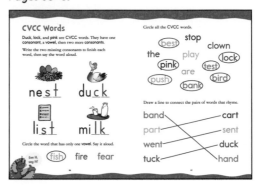

**CVCC Words**

**Duck**, **lock**, and **pink** are CVCC words. They have one **consonant**, a **vowel**, then two more **consonants**.

Write the two missing consonants to finish each word, then say the word aloud.

ne**st**  du**ck**

li**st**  mi**lk**

Circle the word that has only one **vowel**. Say it aloud.

(fish)  fire  fear

Circle all the CVCC words.

(best)  stop
the  play  clown
(pink)  are  (lock)
(push)  (test)
(bank)  (bird)

Draw a line to connect the pairs of words that rhyme.

band — hand
part — cart
went — sent
tuck — duck

## Pages 88–89

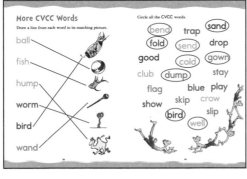

**More CVCC Words**

Draw a line from each word to its matching picture.

ball
fish
hump
worm
bird
wand

Circle all the CVCC words.

(bend)  trap  (sand)
(fold)  (send)  drop
good  (cold)  (gown)
club  (dump)  stay
flag  blue  play
show  skip  crow
(bird)  slip
(well)

## Page 90

**Go, Go, Go!**

Find a path from **START** to **END**. You can only go through real words.

You are smart. You are brilliant.
You are clever, indeed.

## HOORAY FOR

NAME

who is learning to read!

# Phonics Level 2

CERTIFICATE OF ACHIEVEMENT